OF THE HIGHEST GOOD

Boethius of Dacia

Translated by: D.P. Curtin

Dalcassian Publishing Company
PHILADELPHIA, PA

Copyright @ 2007 Dalcassian Publishing Company

All rights reserved. No part of this publication may be reproduced, distributed, or transmitted in any form or by any means, including photocopying, recording, or other electronic or mechanical methods, without the prior written permission of the publisher, except in the case of brief quotations embodied in critical reviews and certain other non-commercial uses permitted by copyright law. For permission request, write to Dalcassian Publishing Company at dalcassianpublishing at gmail.com

ISBN: 979-8-8692-6283-7 (Paperback)

Library of Congress Control Number:
Author: Curtin, D.P. (1985-)

Printed by Ingram Content Group, 1 Ingram Blvd, La Vergne, Tennessee

First printing edition 2007.

OF THE HIGHEST GOOD

    Since in every species of being there is the highest possible good, and since man is a species of being, it must be that some part of the highest good is possible for man. I do not mean the highest good absolutely, but the highest in itself, for the good possible to man has an end and does not proceed to infinity. But what this supreme good is, which is possible to man, let us investigate by reason. The highest good that is possible to man is owed to him according to his best virtue. For not according to the vegetative soul, which is of plants, nor according to the sensitive soul, which is of beasts, whence also the sensible pleasures of beasts. But the best virtue of man is reason and understanding. For it is the supreme rule of human life both in speculating and in working. Therefore, the highest good that is possible to man is owed to himself according to his understanding. And this idea must grieve men who are confined only to sensual pleasures that they omit intellectual goods, because they never reach their highest good. For they are so devoted to the senses that they do not seek what is the good of the intellect itself. Against whom the Philosopher exclaims, saying: "Woe unto you men who are numbered among the beasts, not considering that which is divine in you!" But the Divine in man calls the understanding; For if there is something divine in man, it is worthy that this should be the understanding. For just as that which is best in the whole universe of beings is divine, so we call that which is best in man divine.

Further, since the human intellect has one speculative and another practical power, which is evident from the fact that man is speculative of some of which he is not active, such as the eternal, and of some he is also active according to the government of the intellect through which he works as an eligible medium in all human actions, from this we know that these two intellectual powers exist in man in general. Now the highest good that is possible to man according to the speculative power of the intellect is the knowledge of the truth and the delight in it. For the knowledge of the truth is delightful. For the understanding delights the understanding, and the more the understanding is wonderful and the more noble, and the more the comprehending intellect is of greater power in comprehending perfectly, so much the greater is the intellectual delight. And he who has tasted such a pleasure rejects every lesser as sensible, which in truth is lesser and inferior. And the man who chooses it because of it is cheaper than he who chooses the first. Hence, from the fact that it pleases the understanding, the Philosopher wants understanding in all things. Metaphysics says that the intellect first has the apex of human life. For since the intellect is the first of the greatest powers in understanding, and the intelligible that it understands is the most noble because it is its own essence—for what noble can the divine intellect understand what the divine essence is?—therefore it has the most voluptuous life. Hence, since no greater good can befall man through the speculative intellect than the knowledge of the universe of beings which are from first principles, and through this first principle, as is possible, and delight in it, then it follows that what was concluded above, that the highest good, which is possible for man according to the speculative understanding, there is knowledge of the truth in each individual and delight in the same.

Likewise, the highest good that is possible for man according to practical understanding is the activity of good and delight in the same. For what greater good can befall a man according to practical understanding than to work as an eligible medium in all human activities and to delight in them? For he is not righteous except he who delights in the works of righteousness. And in the same way we must understand the works of the other moral virtues.

OF THE HIGHEST GOOD

From what has been said, it can be clearly concluded that the highest good that is possible for man is the knowledge of the truth and the action of good, and delight in both.

And because the highest good that is possible to man is his happiness, it follows that the knowledge of truth and the activity of good, and delight in both, is human happiness. For this reason the military art was ordered in the city by the legislator, so that the citizens, having expelled their enemies, may spend their time contemplating the truth with their intellectual virtues, and doing good with their moral virtues, and live a happy life. for a happy life consists of these two things. For this is the greatest good that man can receive from God and that God can give to man in this life. And that man desires a reasonably long life, who desires it for this reason, that he may render himself more perfect in this good. For he who is more perfect in happiness than it is possible for man to be in this life by reason, is himself nearer to the happiness which we expect in life to come by faith. And since there is only so much good possible to man, as has already been said, it is fitting that all human actions should be directed towards him, so that they may conclude him. For just as all actions in the loge are in some ways right and as they should be, when they tend to the end of the law, and are better according as they are nearer to the end of the law, but actions which are contrary to the end of the law, or which are diminished—not perfect according to the precepts of the law—or even indifferent— that is to say, neither contrary to the purpose of the law nor according to the precepts of the law - all such actions are sin in that law, according to more and less, as can be seen from what has been said, so it is in man, because all the intentions and plans, actions and desires of man that tend to this The highest good that is possible for man, as has already been said, are right and according to what is necessary. And when a man works in this way, he works naturally, because he works for the sake of the highest good for which he was born. And when he works in this way he is well ordered, because then he is ordered to his best and ultimate end. Now all the actions of man which are not directed to this good, or which are not of such a kind, by which man is rendered stronger and more disposed to actions which are directed to this good, are sin in man. Hence a happy man does nothing but the works of happiness, or the works by which he is rendered stronger or more capable of the works of happiness. Therefore the happy, whether he sleeps or watches or eats, the happy lives, so long as he does these things, that he may be made stronger for the works of happiness.

OF THE HIGHEST GOOD

Hence all the actions of man, which are not directed to this supreme good of man, which has already been said, whether they are opposed to him or are indifferent, are sin in man, according to more and less, as is evident from himself. And the cause of all these actions is disordered concupiscence, which is also the cause of all evil in character. Even man's disordered concupiscence itself is the main cause that hinders man from what he naturally desires. For while all men naturally desire to know, yet very few men, of whom there is sorrow, waste their time in the pursuit of wisdom, and their inordinate concupiscence hinders them from so much good. For we see once the laziness of life, and some detestable sensual pleasures, and once the desire of good fortune. And thus all men today are hindered by inordinate concupiscence from their highest good, with the exception of the very few honorable men; whom I call to be honored, because they despise the desire of the senses and follow the pleasure and desire of the intellect, sweating the knowledge of the truth of things; whom I should also honor with my voice, because they live according to the natural order. For just as all the inferior virtues which are in man naturally exist because of the supreme virtue—for it is nutritive because of the sensitive, in that the sensitive is the perfection of an animated body, and the animated body is not powerful without nourishment, but the nourishing virtue is that which alters and converts the nourishment , because of which it happens that the nutritive in man is because of the sensitive. But it is sensitive because it is intellectual, inasmuch as they are understood in us from what is imagined; therefore we understand with difficulty those things which in themselves cannot have an imagined existence in us. But the imagination does not comprehend until after the sense, the proof of which is, because everyone who imagines is sensibly affected. Hence, according to the Philosopher, imagination or fantasy is a movement made from sense according to act—so the operations of all the lower virtues that are in man are due to the operations of the supreme virtue, which is the intellect. And among the operations of the intellectual power, if any is the best and most perfect, all are naturally || because of her and when man is in that operation, he is in the best state that is possible for man. And these are the philosophers who devote their lives to the study of wisdom. Hence all the virtues which are in the philosopher work according to the natural order: the former for the sake of the latter, and the lower for the sake of the higher and more perfect. But all other men who live according to the lower virtues, choosing the activities and pleasures that are in those activities, are unnaturally ordered and sin against the natural order. For man's deviation from the natural order is a sin in man, and because the philosopher does not deviate from this order, on this account he does not sin against the natural order.

He is also a virtuous philosopher, speaking morally, for three reasons. One thing is that he himself knows the baseness of action in which vice consists, and the nobility of action in which virtue consists, therefore he can more easily choose one of these and avoid the other and always act according to the right reason, who when he acts in this way never sins. But this does not happen to the ignorant, for it is difficult for the ignorant to act rightly. The second reason is that he who has tasted greater pleasure rejects all lesser pleasure. But the philosopher tasted intellectual delight in speculating on the truths of beings, which is greater than the delight of the senses. Therefore, he rejects sensible pleasures. And there are many sins and vices in the excess of sensible pleasure. The third is that there is no sin in understanding and speculating, for in simply good things there is no possible excess and sin; and the action of the philosopher is the speculation of truth; therefore, a philosopher is more easily virtuous than another.

Therefore the philosopher lives as man is born to live and according to the natural order, since all the lower virtues in him and their actions are because of the superior virtues and their actions, and all universally because of the supreme virtue and ultimate action, which is the contemplation of truth and delight in it, and especially of the first truth; for the appetite for knowledge is never satisfied until the uncreated being is known. For the question of the divine understanding is naturally desired to be known by all men, as the Commentator says. For the desire of every knowable is a certain desire of the first knowable, the proof of which is that the more beings come nearer to the first knowable, the more we desire to know them, and the more we are obliged to observe them. For this reason, the philosopher, by speculating on the caused beings which are in the world, and their natures and their order, is brought into the speculating of the deepest causes of things, because the knowledge of effects is a kind of manual induction into the knowledge of their cause. and knowing that the higher causes and their natures are such that it is necessary for them to have another cause, he is brought into the knowledge of the first cause. And the greater pleasure consists in speculating, when they are intelligible and nobler. Therefore, the philosopher leads a very voluptuous life. The philosopher also knows and considers that it is necessary for this reason to be the reason for his own existence, that is, to have no other reason; for if there were nothing in the world that did not have another cause, there would be nothing universally.

OF THE HIGHEST GOOD

Considering also that it is necessary for this cause to be eternal and unchangeable, always having itself in one way, for if it were not eternal, nothing universally would be eternal. And again, since there are certain new things in the world, and one new thing cannot be the sufficient cause of another new thing, as is self-evident, it clearly follows that all the new things that are in the world are universally due to an eternal cause. And the cause is also unchangeable, always having itself in one way, because change is not possible except in imperfect things, and if there is any being that is most perfect in the world, it is worthy that this should be the first cause.

Considering also that the whole being of the world, which is on this side of this first cause, must be from it, and that just as this first cause is the cause of the production of beings, so also of their organization to || the change and preservation of their being, some according to their number and without any change, as separate substances, and some according to their number, yet with change, as the bodies of heaven, and some according to their species only, as are those which are under the world, as They are the lowest level of beings.

Considering also that as all things are from this first cause, so all things are directed to it; for that being in which the beginning, from which all things, is united to the end, to which all things are, this is the first being, according to the philosophers and according to the saints, the blessed god. In this order, however, there is breadth, and the beings which are more closely related in this order in the first principle, are beings more noble and perfect in the image. But those which are in this order more removed from the first principle, are to me beings more diminished and less perfect. For this is the first principle in this world, as the head of the household in the house, and the leader in the army, and the common good in the city. And as the army is one from the unity of the leader, and the good of the army is by itself in the leader, and in others it is according to the order they have to the leader, so from the unity of the ground of the first principle is the unity of this world, and the good of this world is in itself in this first in the beginning, and in other beings of the world according to participation from this first principle and order to it, so that there is no good in any being in the world unless it is shared by this first principle. The philosopher, considering all these things, is led to wonder at this first principle and to love it, because we love that from which our goods proceed, and we especially love that from which our greatest goods proceed. Therefore, the philosopher knowing that all his goods come to him from this first principle and are preserved for him in so far as they are preserved, he is led by this first principle into the greatest love of this first principle, both according to the right reason of nature and according to the right reason of the intellect. And since everyone delights in that which he loves and delights most in that which he loves most, and the philosopher has the greatest love for the first principle, as has been declared, it follows that the philosopher delights most in the first principle and in the contemplation of his goodness. And this is the only true pleasure. This is the life of the philosopher, and whoever does not have it does not have the right life. Now I call a philosopher every man who lives according to the right order of nature, and who has acquired the best and ultimate end of human life. Now the first principle of which the discourse was made is the glorious and exalted God, who is blessed forever and ever. Amen.

LATIN TEXT

Cum in omni specie entis sit aliquod summum bonum possibile, et homo quaedam est species entis, oportet quod aliquod summum bonum sit homim possibile. Non dico summum bonum absolute, sed summum sibi, bona enim possibila homini finem habent nec procedunt in infinitum. Quid autem sit hoc summum bonum, quod est homini possibile, per rationem investigemus. Summum bonum quod est homini possibile debetur sibi secundum optimam suam virtutem. Non enim secundum animam vegetativam, quae plantarum est, nec secundum animam sensitivam quae bestiarum est, unde et delectationes sensibiles bestiarum sunt. Optima autem virtus hominis ratio et intellectus est; est enim summum regimen vitae humanae tam in speculando quam in operando. Ergo summum bonum quod est homini possibile debetur sibi secundum intellectum. Et idea dolere debent homines qui tantum delectationibus sensibilibus detinentur quod bona intellectualia omittunt, quia suum summum bonum numquam attingunt; tantum enim sunt dediti sensibus quod non quaerunt quod est bonum ipsius intellectus. Contra quos exclamat Philosophus dicens: "Vae vobis homines qui computati estis in numero bestiarum ei quod in vobis divinum est non intendentes!" Divinum autem in homine vocat intellectum; si enim in homine aliquid divinum est, dignum est quod hoc sit intellectus. Sicut enim quod in tota universitate entium optimum est hoc divinum est, ita et quod in homine optimum est hoc divinum vocamus.

Praeterea, cum intellectus humani una sit potentia speculativa et alia practica, quod apparet ex hoc quod homo quorundam est speculativus quorum non est activus, ut aeternorum, et quorundam etiam est activus secundum regimen intellectus per quod operatur medium eligibile in omnibus actionibus humanis, ex hoc scimus has duas potentias intellectuales in genere esse in homine. Summum autem bonum quod est homini possibile secundum potentiam intellectus speculativam est cognitio veri et delectatio in eodem. Nam cognitio veri delectabilis est. Intellectum enim delectat intellegentem, et quanto intellectum magis fuerit mirabile et magis nobile, et quanto intellectus comprehendens fuerit maioris virtutis in comprehendendo perfecte, tanto delectatio intellectualis est maior. Et qui gustavit talem delectationem spernit omnem minorem ut sensibilem, quae in veritate minor est et vilior. Et homo qui eam eligit propter eam vilior est, quam qui eligit primam. Unde ex hoc quod intellectum delectat intellegentem vult Philosophus in XI. Metaphysicae quod intellectus primus vitam habet voluptuosissimam. Cum enim intellectus primus sit maximae virtutis in intellegendo, intellegibile autem quod intellegit sit nobilissimum quia sui ipsius essentia—quid enim nobilus potest intellectus divinus intellegere quam sit essentia divina?—ideo habet vitam voluptuosissimam. Unde cum nullum maius bonum possit homini contingere per intellectum speculativum quam cognitio universitatis entium quae sunt a prima principia et per hoc primi principii, sicut possibile est, et delectatio in illa, tunc sequitur quod superius conclusum est, quod summum bonum, quod est homini possibile secundum intellectum speculativum, est cognitio veri in singulis et delectatio in eadem.

Item, summum bonum quod est homini possibile secundum intellectum practicum est operatio boni et delectatio in eadem. Quid enim maius bonum potest homini contingere secundum intellectum practicum quam operari medium eligibile in omnibus actionibus humanis et in illa delectari? Non enim est iustus nisi qui in operibus iustitiae delectatur. Et eadem modo intellegendum est de operibus aliarum virtutum moralium.

Ex his quae dicta sunt manifeste concludi potest quod summum bonum quod est homini possibile est cognitio veri et operatio boni et delectatio in utroque.

Et quia summum bonum quod est homini possibile est eius beatitudo, || sequitur quod cognitio veri et operatio boni et delectatio in utroque sit beatitudo humana. Propter hoc enim ars militaris ordinata est in civitate a legislatore, ut expulsis hostibus cives possint vacare virtutibus intellectualibus contemplantes verum et virtutibus moralibus operantes bonum et vivant vitam beatam; in his enim duobus consistit vita beata. Hoc enim est maius bonum quod homo a deo recipere potest et quod deus homini dare potest in hac vita. Et ille homo rationabiliter longam vitam desiderat, qui eam propter hoc desiderat, ut perfectiorem se reddat in hoc bono. Qui enim perfectior est in beatitudine, quam in hac vita homini possibile esse per rationem scirnus, ipso propinquior est beatitudini quam in vita futura per fidem expectamus. Et cum tantum bonum sit homini possibile, sicut jam dictum est, dignum est ut omnes actiones humanae in ipsum dirigantur, ut ipsum concludant. Sicut enim omnes actiones in loge aliqua rectae sunt et ut oportet, cum tendunt in finem legis, et meliores secundum quod fini legis propinquiores, actiones autem, quae adversantur fini legis, vel quae deminutae sunt—non perfectae secundum praecepta legis—vel etiam indifferentes—scilicet nec oppositae fini legis nec secundum praecepta legis— omnes tales actiones peccatum sunt in lege illa, secundum tamen magis et minus, ut patere potest ex dictis, sic est in homine, quia omnes intentiones et consilia, actiones et desideria hominis quae tendunt

OF THE HIGHEST GOOD

in hoc summum bonum, quod est homini possibile, quod iam dictum est, recta sunt et secundum quod oportet. Et cum homo sic operatur, naturaliter operatur, quia operatur propter summum bonum ad quod innatus est. Et cum operatur sic bene ordinatus est, quia tunc ordinatur ad optimum et ultimum suum finem. Omnes autem actiones hominis quae non ordinantur ad hoc bonum vel quae non sunt tales, per quas homo redditur fortior et magis diapositus ad operationes, quae ordinantur ad hoc bonum, peccatum sunt in homme. Unde homo felix nihil operatur nisi opera felicitatis vel opera per quae redditur fortior vel magis habilis ad opera felicitatis. Ideo felix sive dormiat sive vigilet sive comedat, felicitor vivit, dummodo illa facit, ut reddatur fortior ad opera felicitatis.

Unde omnes actiones hominis, quae non diriguntur in hoc summum bonum hominis, quod iam dictum est, sive opponantur sibi, sive sint indifferentes, peccatum sunt in homine, secundum tamen magis et minus, ut patet ex se. Et omnium illarum actionum causa est inordinata concupiscentia, quae etiam est causa omnis mali in moribus. Inordinata etiam concupiscentia hominis ipsa est causa maxime impediens hominem a suo desiderate naturaliter. Cum enim omnes homines naturaliter scire desiderant, paucissimi tamen hominum, de quo dolor est, studio sapientiae vacant inordinata concupiscentia eos a tanto bono impediente. Videmus enim quondam pigritiam vitae sequi, quosdam autem voluptates sensibiles detestabiles et quondam desiderium bonorum fortunae. Et ita omnes hominen hodie impedit inordinata concupiscentia a suo summo bono exceptis paucissimis honorandis viris; quos voco honorandos, quia contemnunt desiderium sensus et sequuntur delectationem et desiderium intellectus insudantes cognitioni veritatis rerum; quos etiam voce honorandem, quia vivunt secundum ordinem naturalem. Nam sicut omnes virtutes inferiores, quae sunt in homine, naturaliter sunt propter virtutem supremam—nutritiva enim est propter sensitivam, eo quod sensitiva perfectio est corporis cuiusdam animati, corpus autem animatum non potent esse sine nutrimento, nutritiva autem virtus est quae nutrimentum alterat et convertit, propter quod contingit quod nutritiva in homine sit propter sensitivam. Sensitiva autem est propter intellectivam, eo quod intellecta in nobis sunt ex imaginatis, ideo difficilius illa intellegimus, quae secundum se esse imaginatum habere non possunt in nobis. Imaginatio autem non comprehendit nisi post sensum, cuius probatio est, quia omnis imaginans sensibiliter afficitur. Unde secundum Philosophum imaginatio sive phantasia est motus factus ex sensu secundum actum—sic operationes omnium virtutum inferiorum quae sunt in homine sunt propter operationes virtutis supremae, quae est intellectus. Et inter operationes virtutis intellectivae, si aliqua est optima et perfectissima, omnes naturaliter sunt || propter illam. Et cum homo est in illa operatione, est in optimo statu qui est homini possibilis. Et isti sunt philosophi, qui ponunt vitam suam in studio sapientiae. Unde omnes virtutes quae sunt in philosopho operantur secundum ordinem naturalem: prior propter posteriorem et inferior propter superiorem et perfectiorem. Omnes autem alii homines qui vivunt secundum virtutes inferiores eligentes operationes enim et delectationes, quae sunt in illis operibus, innaturaliter ordinati sunt et peccant contra ordinem naturalem. Declinatio enim hominis ab ordine naturali peccatum est in homine, et quia philosophus ab hoc ordine non declinat, propter hoc contra ordinem naturalem non peccat.

Est etiam philosophus virtuosus moraliter loquendo propter tria. Unum est quod ipse cognoscit turpitudinem actionis, in qua consistit vitium, et nobilitatem actionis, in qua consistit virtus, ideo facilius potest eligere unum istorum et vitare reliquum et semper agere secundum rectam rationem, qui cum sic agit numquam peccat. Hoc autem non contingit ignoranti, nam ignorantem grave est recte agere. Secundum est quia qui gustavit delectationem maiorem spernit omnem delectationem minorem; philosophus autem gustavit delectationem intellectualem in speculando veritates entium, quae est maior quam delectatio sensus; ideo spernit delectationes sensibiles. Et plura peccata et vitia sunt in excessu delectationis sensibilis. Tertium est quia in intellegendo et speculando non est peccatum, in simpliciter enim bonis non est possibilis excessus et peccatum; actio autem philosophi est speculatio veritatis; ideo philosophus est facilius virtuosus quam alius.

Ideo philosophus vivit sicut homo innatus est vivere et secundum ordinem naturalem, cum onmes virtutes in eo inferiores et actiones earum sint propter virtutes superiores et actiones earum, et omnes universaliter propter virtutem supremam et actionem ultimam, quae est speculatio veritatis et delectatio in illa, et praecipue veritatis primae; numquam enim satiatur appetitus sciendi, donec sciatur ens increatum. Quaestio enim de intellectu divino est naturaliter sciri desiderata ab omnibus hominibus, ut dicit Commentator. Desiderium enim cuiuslibet scibilis est aliquod desiderium primi scibilis, cuius probatio est quod quanto entia magis appropinquant primo scibili, tanto magis illa scire desideramus, et tanto magis in speculatione eorum debetamur. Ideo philosophus speculando entia causata, quae sunt in mundo, et naturas eorum et ordinem eorum ad invicem inducitur in speculationem altissimarum causarum rerum, quia cognitio effectuum est quaedam manuductio in cognitionem suae causae; et cognoscens causas superiores et naturas earum esse tales, quod necesse est eas habere aliam causam, inducitur in cognitionem primae causae. Et in speculando consistit delectatio et maior, cum intellegibilia sint nobiliora. Ideo philosophus ducit vitam valde voluptuosam. Philosophus etiam cognoscens et considerans quod necesse est hanc causam esse sibi ipsi causam essendi, hoc est aliam causam non habere; si enim in mundo nihil esset quod aliam causam non haberet, universaliter nihil esset.

Considerans etiam quod necesse est hanc causam esse aeternam et incommutabilem, semper uno modo se habentem, si enim ipsa non esset aeterna, universaliter nihil esset aeternum. Et iterum cum quaedam in mundo sint entia nova, et unum novum non potest esse causa sufficiens alterius novi, ut ex se patet, sequitur manifeste quod omnia nova quae sunt in mundo universaliter sunt ex causa aeterna. Et causa etiam est incommutabilis semper uno modo se habens, quia transmutatio non est possibilis nisi in rebus imperfectis, et si aliquod est ens perfectissimum in mundo, dignum est quod hoc sit prima causa.

Considerans etiam quod necesse est totum ens mundi, quod est citra hanc primam causam, esse ex ipsa, et quod sicut haec prima causa est causa productionis entium, sic et ordinationis eorum ad in || vicem et conservationis eorum in esse, quorundam secundum suum numerum et sine omni transmutatione, sicut substantiarum separatarum, et quorundam secundum numerum suum, tamen cum transmutatione, sicut corporum caeli, et quorundam secundum suam speciem tantum, sicut sunt illa quae sub orbe sunt, sicut sunt infimus gradus entium.

Considerans etiam quod sicut omnia sunt ex hac prima causa, sic omnia ad ipsam ordinantur; nam ens illud in quo principium, a quo omnia, coniungitur fini, ad quem omnia, hoc est ens primum secundum philosophos et secundum sanctos deus benedictus. In hoc tamen ordine latitudo est, et entia, quae in hoc ordine primo principio magis sunt propinqua, sunt entia nobiliora et imagis perfecta. Quae autem sunt in hoc ordine magis remota a primo principio, me sunt entia magis deminuta et minus perfecta. Est enim hoc primum principium in hoc mundo sicut paterfamilias in domo et dux in exercitu et bonum commune in civitate. Et sicut exercitus est unus ab unitate ducis, et bonum exercitus per se est in duce, in aliis autem est secundum ordinem quem habent ad ducem, sic ex unitate humus primi principii est unitas huius mundi, et bonum huius mundi per se est in hoc primo principio, in aliis autem entibus mundi secundum participationem ab hoc primo principio et ordinem ad ipsum, ut nullum sit bonum in aliquo ente mundi, nisi sit ab hoc primo principio participatum. Philosophus haec omnia considerans inducitur in admirationem huius primi principii et in amorem eius, quia nos amamus illud a quo nobis bona proveniunt, et maxime id amamus a quo nobis maxima bona proveniunt. Ideo philosophus cognoscens omnia sua bona sibi provenire ex hoc primo principio et sibi conservari, quantum conservantur, per hoc primum principium inducitur in maximum amorem huius primi principii et secundum rectam rationem naturae et secundum rationem rectam intellectualem. Et quia quilibet delectatur in illo quod amat et maxime delectatur in illo quod maxime amat, et philosophus maximum amorem habet primi principii, sicut declaratum est, sequitur quod philosophus in primo principio maxime delectatur et in contemplatione bonitatis suae. Et haec sola est recta delectatio. Haec est vita philosophi, quam quicumque non habuerit non habet rectam vitam. Philosophum autem voco omnem hominem viventem secundum rectum ordinem naturae, et qui acquisivit optimum et ultimum finem vitae humanae. Primum autem principium, de quo sermo factus est, est deus gloriosus et sublimis, qui est benedictus in saecula saeculorum. Amen.

The Scriptorium Project is the work of a small group of lay people of various apostolic churches who are interested in the preservation, transmission, and translation of the works of the early and medieval church. Our efforts are to make the works of the church fathers accessible to anyone who might have an interest in Christian antiquities and the theological, philosophical, and moral writings that have become the bedrock of Western Civilization.

To-date, our releases have pulled from the Greek, Syriac, Georgian, Latin, Celtic, Ethiopian, and Coptic traditions of Christianity, and have been pulled from sundry local traditions and languages.

www.ingramcontent.com/pod-product-compliance
Lightning Source LLC
LaVergne TN
LVHW061044070526
838201LV00073B/5174